# Healing Meditations from the Gospel of St. John

## The Psychological and Spiritual Search for the True Self

Dr. Ross Porter
with
Ronda Chervin

ISBN #1-891280-07-4

Library of Congress Catalog Card Number #99-091371

Publisher:
CMJ Marian Publishers
Post Office Box 661
Oak Lawn, Illinois  60454
www.cmjbooks.com
jwby@aol.com

Manufactured in the United States of America

# Contents

# Opening

Toward the end of his life, someone asked Thomas Merton for advice on how to live. The contemplative responded, "Be who you are."

On the surface this may sound absurd . . . we need to change, to grow, to be more and more real. No doubt, however, the journey is not a search "out there," but rather a return to our homes, our hearts.

*Healing Meditations from the Gospel of St. John* is about recovering who we are . . . our true selves. Simply put, the true self is the self that God wants us to be, what Kierkegaard called God's prophesy for each person, gifts, potentialities, feelings . . . all that our Creator originally gave us as images of God.

As co-authors seeking wisdom about the nature of the true self, one a philosophical and spiritual writer, the other a psychologist, it was natural to turn to the Gospel of St. John. After all, it was St. John who was Christ's "beloved disciple". . . the one to whom Jesus turned as he hung on the cross, entrusting his own mother to him.

It is our hope that *Healing Meditations from the Gospel of St. John* will be nourishing for some of the many Christians we meet every day who want to find truths that help them as spiritual seekers, and who are yet emotionally wounded, who want like we do to be healed in our personalities as mind, body, heart, and spirit come together. Each chapter begins with a selection from the Gospel of St. John, followed by a teaching, reflection questions, and then a guided imagery. It is suggested that you read our Healing Meditations slowly in a quiet place.

Our book is not a substitute for psychotherapy or for spiritual direction. Its intended purpose is to be either a supplement or an entry point to more individual healing. We pray that it may be a source of encouragement and hope for all who read it.

T. S. Eliot writes,

We shall not cease from exploration
And the end of all our exploring
Will be to arrive where we started
And know the place for the first time.

# I
# John 1:1–5 The Prologue

## The True Self Created by God

In the beginning was the Word:
and the Word was with God:
and the Word was God.
The same was in the beginning with God.
All things were made by him: and without him
was made nothing that was made.
In him was life: and the life was the light of men.
And the light shineth in darkness:
and the darkness did not comprehend it.

(John 1: 1-5)

The beginning of the prologue to the Gospel of St. John holds wonderful images for discovering our true selves on deeper and deeper levels.

Let's start with the Word. . .eternal Logos. . .ultimate source of creativity, and meaning; the Word must be where a search for the true self begins. In our first chapter we will explore some of the most foundational aspects of the true self in its relation to God. In later chapters each of these insights will be amplified.

Starting with the Word as Source of the self immediately keeps the seeker from imagining that the self is some interior reality completely independent of God. Even

1

though such imagery is suggestive it is not really the case that we can get to the true self simply by peeling off layers of false selves as if they were onion skins or, to bring in the sense of taste, by licking off rounds of hard lollipop to get to the tootsie roll inside!

Whatever the true self will turn out to be, the Holy Spirit through St. John teaches us that we are intimately linked to our creative source: The Word, without whom nothing came into being.

The true self is a child of a Fathering being, not something utterly private even from its creator as extreme individualism would imagine. And, in fact, there is an Adam-after-the-Fall part of each of us that would like to hide even from the creator of our true selves. We come in touch with this fallen-Adam part of ourselves whenever we run from deep meeting with God in prayer, as if assuming that our true self will just be there in some treasure chest "inside" the soul waiting for us to take an interest in it!

We must keep bearing this in mind as we respond to the two surprising images that jump out at the reader immediately in the Gospel passage: life and light. When we are living in our true selves, that is the self God made each of us to be, we are life giving. We are dynamic, magnetic, and incredibly creative. We seem to shine, to "glow," to radiate light, and we feel more light-hearted than usual. Picture a pianist reaching the peak of a crescendo with lightening speed, or a diver plunging from a spectacular new height into the water below, or a parent enfolding a new born babe in his or her embrace.

Although the sight of a person actualizing his or her highest potentialities may be dramatic to the viewer, the creative energy within the person flows from a quiet center of life quite different than when we act out of compulsive need to make an effect, to produce, to perform only to win applause. Hence the sweet shy look of the truly creative person when the applause does come, not because it was sought as the number one goal but as a reverberation of the acting person's own pulsating focussed energy in the hands of the clapping audience.

The sense of life and light coming from the true self is sometimes expressed metaphysically in the notion that it is important to value being more than doing. The ideal expressed in this somewhat enigmatic formula is not one of being in a coma as preferable to engaging in passionate action. What we want to suggest is that there is an interior goodness of selfhood, a still point in the turning world as T. S. Eliot wrote, an innermost "me," that is in the image and likeness of God. It is this true self that is joined by an invisible umbilical cord to our creator.

And it is Christ, the Creative Word, who wants to water that seed of true selfhood, who wants to nurture it gently if we will let him in through prayer and meditation on his self-revelation in Scripture.

When we do *not* know our own true selves, where light emerges out of the life we have been given by God, we waste a lot of time in frantic doings. We seek to "see" ourselves in the mirror of the approving eyes of other human beings. We fall into patterns of "people pleasing," so desperate that we become slaves.

We all know of those who cannot feel beautiful in their bodies until a certain quota of complimentary remarks has flattered their ears. "Oh, you look gorgeous tonight." "My God, I thought you were 25, you can't be a woman with grandchildren!" "You look so fit I thought maybe you were a professional athlete."

If we live mainly in our heads we may laugh at such a need for superficial affirmation, yet aren't we just as mistaken thinking that the value of a poem we wrote depends on the number of reviewers who approved of it? Or that our worth is measured by our paycheck?

In the course of meditating on the Gospel of St. John we will begin to know the healing that he experienced in his own self in being so close to the Lord Jesus. We will come to feel more interested in the desires of one Person. . .the second member of the Trinity. . .who creates, redeems, and sanctifies our true self, and in whose love we come to know a self previously hidden even from ourselves. We will recognize this self as the one of which we have gotten fleeting glimpses in the past.

For many Christians, having a prayer-time each day or going to daily Mass is a means of confirming the right of the true self to "prime time" in the day. Out of this place of peace we want to move outward in our true selves to whatever confronts us during the rest of the day.

Light. The Psalmist writes, "For with you is the fountain of life, and in your light we see light." (Psalm 36: 10) There is wisdom and a deep sense of discernment that accompanies those who seek Jesus first.

Their life, their creative power is illumined by the light of the Word, which may be why so many have seen an aura of light around the faces and whole bodies of holy men and women.

The light of Christ shines even through the darkest hours as when a man struggles all day with a migraine headache, nonetheless reaching out to others with sweetness and humor. There is a light that shines through the darkness of mental breakdown when in spite of dread and despair, a woman hangs onto a faint light of hope at the end of the seemingly interminable tunnel of her terrifying inner life. The man with the pounding head has to believe that his true self is more than his pain. The woman shattered in her emotional equilibrium has to believe that new life can grow from a self deeper than the disturbing images and fantasies that have overcome all reason and peace.

As we strive to discover who it is that God wants us to be, and how He is asking us to invest our lives, our energies, we must lean on Jesus, who is the Way, and the Truth, and the Life. Developing spiritually and psychologically, living more and more in our true selves, is a journey powered by God's grace.

It takes courage to accept the fact that we cannot just conjure up a true self, through brute willpower, as if we were totally self-sufficient. We cannot create the light that shows us the way to wholeness. We must wait on the Lord to give us the gift of illumination.

This waiting is far from passive, though. It calls us to lay aside from time to time the activities that give us a pseudo-sense of self-possession because we can succeed easily at them, in order to come to Christ in prayer, and to reach out to brothers and sisters in Christ in all vulnerability.

The most important way to prepare for healing through meditation on the Gospel of St. John will be, then, to set aside a quiet time for reading, writing responses, speaking with friends. We have to silence the compulsive voice within telling us to "just finish this job or chore first" or "don't waste time on the spiritual — you have your old age for that, now you have to forge ahead to keep up. . . ."

Sometimes when we read paragraphs like the last one we can become discouraged. "Well, if I can only find my true self by becoming an introspective recluse, forget it!" or "Sure, sometimes my emotions get out of control, but still they are a part of the real me and I don't want to become numb by cutting off half my vital energies to tune out reality."

As you read on you will see that the authors of this book are not pushing onto you such a truncated image of authentic selfhood. In recommending a choice for a time of silence and reflection we are hoping to channel your anxiety into yearning for a self whose emotions are full of real life instead of manic spasmodic spurts of energy; to channel your thoughts until they reflect the light of Christ instead of sparks that die out all too quickly under a blanket of skepticism.

## For Reflection

1. In what ways do you now search for your true self? Describe high points in self-discovery you have already experienced.

2. In what ways do you live your life through other people's eyes? Whose eyes are you most anxious to shine in? How do you feel when you see no affirming response in them?

3. In what specific ways do you try to see yourself in the eyes of your Savior Jesus Christ, the author of meaning?

### *Guided Imagery*

Recognizing that a quiet place is needed to better hear the Holy Spirit's leading, we suggest that you assume now a relaxed position. Remembering that the word for Spirit in Hebrew (ruah) also means breath, in silence become aware of your own breathing.

Ask the Holy Spirit to fall afresh on you and guide you in this inner journey of healing and insight.

Picture an atmosphere of glowing light. Now imagine God the Father in any form you feel comfortable with.

Picture him conferring with his Son about creation. The Father is deciding to create *you*! Listen to him speak your name through the Word. See your true self as a sparkling jewel being formed in the hands of Jesus. If this image does not appeal to you, ask the Holy Spirit to give you one that does.

If none of these images appeal to you, ask the Holy Spirit to give you one that will.

Now picture that true self of yours glowing in the light. The Father and Son are smiling at you.

Now you see the Holy Spirit, as a dove or some form you prefer, lifting up your true self, carrying it and presenting it as a gift to the world.

If you are a baptized person, picture that true self flowing with light as the baptismal water is being poured over you. If you are not baptized picture right now the light coming toward you to illumine still more brightly your true self.

# II
# John 1: 14 The Word Became Flesh

## The True Self as Embodied Spirit

> And the Word was made flesh and dwelt among us
> (and we saw his glory, the glory as it were of the
> only begotten of the Father), full of grace and truth.
>
> (John 1: 14)

The Incarnation; the beautiful Revelation of the God-man... Jesus Christ freely chose to live among us in a human body. He who contained the whole world was willing to exist as a tiny little baby in the womb of Mary. He who could change water into wine was willing to undergo all the daily exigencies of living in a limited body such as needing sleep, feeling hunger and thirst as during the forty days in the desert, and even requiring a digestive system.

Not only is the truth that God became man at the very heart of the Christian faith, it also holds tremendous insight into discovering our true selves. Body and Spirit; not only is it the make-up of our Risen Lord, it is also our composite.

Throughout the ages, some thinkers have tried to call one side, either body or spirit, unreal or certainly less real. Some philosophers believe that only the immaterial spirit is real and the body but an illusory veil. Others think that the body is truly real, and what is called spirit is but an insubstantial construct.

Uneasiness about having to be an embodied spirit, a unique personality expressed in bone and marrow, muscle and skin, can lead to a mistaken notion that one or the other, spirit or flesh, needs to be "overcome."

It is easy to see where that can lead: emphasizing the body while neglecting the spirit can lock someone up in a kind of sensual prison where physical needs have absolute reign. Under the force of substance addictions we can come to believe that any means is justified in satisfying overpowering needs, justified as compensation for deep psychological wounds. . ."if I can just get a physical 'fix' then I do not have to face these wounds."

When we make a fetish of our outward appearance, we also emphasize the body too much; as in spending hours a day on make-up, clothing, or physique.

On the other hand, trying to pretend to be pure spirit by attempts to abandon the body leaves us so "otherworldly" that we are of little earthly good. We imagine that by cultivating an interior life we will become so detached from the world that we will be able to dispense with the body all together. When we become what is sometimes called "spacey," we get so wrapped up in thought and fantasy that we have no focus for taking care of necessities such as earning a living or caring for the young.

Discovering our true selves is intimately tied to finding a balance between body and spirit. When either body or spirit tries to go it alone, the neglected side rises up in conscious or often unconscious battle. Gluttony or promiscuity can lead not to the expected fullness but to emptiness. Could this emptiness be the voice of the neglected spirit crying out for some fulfillment for itself? Or, to use an opposite example, fatigue and pain can be signals of a neglected body crying out for a share in the life of a person who becomes too purely mental.

One of the reasons why we may find it hard to find a balance between body and soul has to do with messages received in youth from family or the wider culture. For many it was the body that was over-stressed as in a strained insistence on rigid patterns of eating and sleeping as if we would starve or die without having exact amounts of food or rest. Over-protective parents can convey the idea that bodily safety has the greatest value, even being more important than eternal life.

A childhood surrounded by addictive adults can also model patterns hard to overcome. While this is fairly obvious in the case of children of alcoholics, it can also be found in the case of more subtle influences toward such goals as perfectionism of appearance, immaculate neatness, the conspicuous flaunting of flashy cars, or even a worship of health and vitality such that sickness or tiredness have to be concealed to put up a good show.

For others, a severe distaste for the body can be conveyed by a horror of bathroom functions; an abiding sense that sexual parts of the body are repulsive or shameful. Fear of punishment for initial childhood exploration of our own bodies or that of others, or shame connected with abuse can sometimes lead to manipulative sexual behavior as adults. Sexual abuse can also result in a desire to leave the body behind in an overly defensive and unhelpful way, trying to center oneself in the realm of the purely spiritual not so much from grace as from fear. Long familiarity with religious people who seemed crazed and out of touch with reality can set a pattern of flight to the practical at the expense of the spirit.

Seeking a balance between body and spirit, we may find that when the less prominent side is given its due the over-emphasized element of the self comes under healthy moderation. When a sedentary person goes into an exercise program, his or her intellectual work may become less congested. When a self-indulgently sensual person spends more time on the search for truth, the sensory side can regain its original innocence.

Recognizing our spiritual dimension allows us the opportunity to transcend, get free of the compulsive traps of this world that can be so seductive. Our spirits remind us that we were built for communion with God, made in His image and eager to develop loving, less exploitative relations with others.

On the other side, for those of us who tend to develop the immaterial at the expense of the physical, it is critical to root our spiritual existence in a healthy incarnationalism. We are "clay vessels," and need to be aware of our physical realities. Is it not a gift of God to find a troublesome intellectual problem unravel after God's gift of a good night's sleep? Could we feel more kindly toward an irritating person after a strolling or swimming break unless our bodies had a lot to do with our souls? The author of the Letter to the Hebrews says we are "temples of the Holy Spirit". . . doesn't it make sense to be attentive to "up-keep" issues such as proper rest, diet, and exercise?

Yes, God in His infinite goodness and wisdom has provided us with a potentially wonderful measure of psychological and spiritual health: the balance we work out between the needs of our bodies and the needs of our spirits. When we live in our true selves, we discover that the apparent "tension" between the body and the spirit is a superficial reading. The body and the spirit actually complement each other, and present the truth of the incarnation in what might first appear to be a riddle: we can only fly when we are properly grounded!

If you think the last thoughts are too idealistic because of the intensity of your struggles with body/spirit issues, we suggest you read the chapters to follow, which may speak to your issues in a more specific way.

## For Reflection

1. Do you find yourself emphasizing either the body or the spirit in your life to the neglect of the other part of the composite? Do you remember any "messages" you got along the way that encouraged you in one direction or the other. . .body or spirit?

2. Are there particular fears you associate with nurturing either the needs of the body or the needs of the Spirit? What dangers do you see in over-emphasizing one or the other? What are the ways you nurture your body and your spirit?

3. Are there personal injuries or traumas you suffered (physical, emotional, spiritual or any combination of these) in your life that might be acting as an obstacle (or obstacles) to a greater balance?

4 What would be one step you could take to achieve greater balance in your daily life between body and spirit, allowing each side to speak to you more of its needs — such as more time for prayer or exercise, better eating habits, etc. An acronym used in twelve step programs might be helpful. HALT reminds us: never too Hungry, never too Angry, never too Lonely, and never too Tired.

### Guided Imagery

Picture the figure of Jesus Christ, the God-man. He is standing at the top of a hill possibly in Galilee. You are walking up the hill toward him. What does he look like? What is the expression in his eyes as he realizes it is you coming toward him? Does he run or walk toward you? Does he stand still waiting? Does he open his arms to receive you, or stand with arms folded on his chest?

When others come toward you physically or emotionally what is your most typical posture? Do you wish that you opened yourself to others in a different posture? If so, ask Jesus to show you how.

# III
# John 2: 1 – 11 The Wedding at Cana

## Becoming One's True Self
## by Surrender to Christ

And the third day, there was a marriage in Cana of
Galilee: and the mother of Jesus was there.
And Jesus also was invited, and his disciples, to the
marriage.
And the wine failing, the mother of Jesus saith to
him: They have no wine.
And Jesus saith to her: Woman, what is that to me and
to thee? My hour is not yet come. What is that to me.
His mother saith to the waiters: Whatsoever he shall
say to you, do ye.
Now there were set there six waterpots of stone, according to the manner of the purifying of the Jews,
containing two or three measures apiece.
Jesus saith to them: Fill the waterpots with water.
And they filled them up to the brim.
And Jesus saith to them: Draw out now and carry to
the chief steward of the feast. And they carried it.
And when the chief steward had tasted the water
made wine and knew not whence it was, but the
waiters knew who had drawn the water: the chief
steward calleth the bridegroom,

And saith to him: Every man at first setteth forth
good wine, and when men have well drunk, then that
which is worse. But thou hast kept the good wine
until now.
This beginning of miracles did Jesus in Cana of Galilee and manifested his glory. And his disciples believed in him.

(John 2: 1 -1 1)

"Do whatever he tells you."
Surrender. What is the first image that comes to mind?
A man waving a white flag, giving up, losing everything!
We would guess many would not consider "surrender" a
positive concept. In a society that prides itself on competi-
tion and "survival of the fittest," "surrender" is kind of
scandalous; it is quickly linked with failure and even anni-
hilation.

As we continue our search for our true selves, living
our lives as God wants us to live, we learn that surrender
to Christ, if understood in the light of the miracle at Cana,
can be one of the most effective ways of breaking
"people-pleasing" compulsions.

The Mother of God shows us the way that surrender
can heal and transform the splintered, injured parts of our
lives. "Do whatever he tells you." It is Who we surrender
to that makes the difference between life and death. If we
surrender to the perfect will of God, recognizing that surrender to God happens in stages and all true changes usually take time to set in, then we slowly begin to see who
we really are. Our true identities are found by looking into
the eyes of Jesus, the Risen Lord, who found us so pre-
cious he was willing to go to Calvary for us.

Life blossoms within us like never before, because we
are beginning to be free — free of the never-ending pressure to live our lives through other people's eyes; free of

the pressure to meet other people's expectations; free of the pressure to be perfect. Of course we still feel angered, saddened, and even momentarily discouraged when others do not approve of us, but such negative responses no longer have the power to devastate, for our selfhood has a worth independent of our image in the eyes of others.

Jesus has done the work on the cross. By overcoming death, He has shown us that like the change He effected by turning water into wine, He can transform us into whole people, full of joy and peace. Even though the process of becoming children of joy and peace may be much slower than we would wish, the glimpses that we get of these positive states of being are enough to give us the hope to want to live closer and closer to the one who can deliver to us such joy and peace. Supernatural hope moves us to explore ways of prayer and patterns of living conducive to greater closeness to the one we call Savior.

If we don't begin the all-important process of surrender to Jesus, a process that begins but does not end when we ask Jesus to be Lord of our lives, He cannot transform our brokenness into holiness.

Why? Because God loves and respects us too much to ever "force" us to surrender. This is the choice He made when He gave us the gift of free choice. In the rhythm of this mystery we sense the aptness of the analogy of the Song of Songs for the bride-soul must surrender to be inseminated and fructified by the groom-Christ.

Refusing to surrender to Jesus, we automatically choose to surrender to the false illusion that we can redeem ourselves by turning head-stands to retain a positive self-image, or that we can be validated by someone else whose affirmation is to become the source of our true selves. This is a path that leads away from the Author of Life. As St. Augustine said, "Do not look for life in the land of death."

Prayer for wisdom is the first step in understanding "how" to surrender to Jesus. Remember, none of us can "do it alone." A competent spiritual director led by the Holy Spirit can help us understand the spiritual issues involved in the journey towards surrender, and our true selves. A Christ-centered, well-trained psychotherapist can help us identify psychological developmental obstacles that might be impeding our journey, beginning with trust issues.

A few examples of others finding their true selves by means of total surrender may give us an impetus to take this risk. St. Jane of Chantal, the spiritual friend of St. Francis de Sales, in the early years when he was directing her, was ardent and dedicated, but had a tendency to put too much trust in her own efforts to sanctify herself through working hard on her faults. The loving discernment of St. Francis eventually helped her to trust only in the love of Jesus, her spouse. An early portrait of St. Jane shows her rather stiff and proud. A later portrait of St. Jane as a Visitation nun shows her eyes almost liquid with the sweetness of surrender.

Another example is St. Alphonsus Liguori. He was a brilliant lawyer, but very arrogant. He was so arrogant that when he lost an important case he abandoned his profession in horror at his failure.

Later when surrendering to God's will that he be a priest ministering to poor mountain folk in a remote region of Italy, we see him evangelizing from the back of a donkey, wearing ragged clothing, oblivious to all appearances, and willing to endure vicious ridicule even from his brethren out of love for Jesus.

## For Reflection

1. What does surrender mean for you?

2. How have you been hurt by "surrendering" to a person (people) other than Jesus?

3. What are some ways you can begin surrendering to Jesus, and "do whatever He tells you to do"?

4. Are you willing to be patient with the transformation process, and "wait on the Lord"? Jesus changed the water into wine quickly, but can you see advantages in "process miracles" that is, miracles that happen more slowly?

5. Write a list of adjectives you use to describe yourself? What are the adjectives about yourself that others use most frequently? When you "look" into the eyes of Jesus, what do you see of yourself?

### *Guided Imagery*

You are at a banquet sitting with Mary. You have a lot on your heart that you want to share, but anxieties seem to block you from letting it out.

You find yourself asking, "what shall I do"? Look at her eyes, full of compassion and love. She seems to understand. What does she say to you? Does she even need to speak?

Now imagine Mary and yourself leaving the table and walking outside of the banquet hall. You see Jesus a short distance away — alone and waiting. What do you feel?

Mary takes you gently by the hand and guides you toward her son. Jesus reaches out to take your other hand. You see in his eyes the same loving response that you saw in his mother and you recognize that Mary has given you her answer: her Son.

Feel the heaviness of your heart begin to lift, the yoke on your shoulders slide off.

You see your circumstances in a new way — as opportunities for growth in communion with God.

Is there a specific care you need to give him now, or is it more a general feeling of distress? He wants to shoulder your cares. Now give him your burden. See the smile on his face and the kindness in his glance.

# IV
# John 2: 13 – 17 Jesus Drives out the Moneychangers

## The Place of Anger in the Discovery of the True Self

And the pasch of the Jews was at hand: and Jesus went up to Jerusalem.
And he found in the temple them that sold oxen and sheep and doves, and the changers of money sitting.
And when he had made, as it were, a scourge of little cords, he drove them all out of the temple, the sheep also and the oxen: and the money of the changers he poured out, and the tables he overthrew.
And to them that sold doves he said: Take these things hence, and make not the house of my Father a house of traffic.
And his disciples remembered, that it was written: The zeal of thy house hath eaten me up.

(John 2: 13-17)

There are very few emotions that have the ability to either build up or tear down faster than anger. Because the bad reasons for anger and the good ones are sometimes so hard to sort out, this chapter will be a little longer than the previous ones.

So many Christians suffer under the false teaching that anger is wrong. . .that it is sin. This conviction is based on Scriptures such as "let not the sun set on your anger," (Ephesians 4:26) or ". . . never lose your temper, or raise your voice to anybody, or call each other names, or allow any sort of spitefulness. Be friends with one another, and kind, forgiving each other as readily as God forgave you in Christ." (Ephesians 4: 30–32)

It is easy to see how we can take such Scriptures to rule out any kind of anger whatsoever, especially if in childhood we were constantly hushed up or told only to say nice things to others. The combination of dutiful piety and this kind of child-rearing can lead us into unhealthy patterns of repression, not only of angry words and deeds but even of angry feelings.

Without the willingness to feel our emotions, our true selves cannot evolve. Yet, naturally, we are afraid of feelings that might get out of control.

A close consideration of Scripture shows us that it is not the immediate feeling of anger, but what we do with the anger, that can be problematic. David's anger at the bullying Goliath was appropriate and led to courageous battling against injustice. His anger, however, at the husband of Bathsheba was understandable but expressed in an evil murderous deed. Even the Lord God himself is occasionally described as being angry with His people.

In cases of response to injustice, anger can even be a virtue and an obligation such as showing anger when someone tortures an innocent victim.

What we have to look at carefully is anger that is out of proportion, out of control, enduring way beyond what is reasonable. Some of us need to remember that cold disdain over years that comes from unwillingness to forgive can be just as wrong as hot anger.

Feeling angry or informing others that their actions make us angry need not always fall under labels such as uncontrolled or out of proportion.

Our perfect model, Jesus, shows us that He certainly became angry. . . and we know that He led a sinless life. We are all going to feel angry from time to time, so the question is not "How can we avoid anger?", but rather, "How can we use anger to discover our true selves?"

Anger is far too complicated to handle with technique alone. We need God's grace. Is there a "rule of thumb" we can carry with us about the expression of anger that will open us to God's grace?

Jesus provides us with the answer: "Take these things away; you will not make my Father's house a house of trade." Indeed, zeal, or passion, for God's house and all that it meant consumed Jesus. His whole ministry was, and continues to be, bringing people into authentic relationship with God. The key question to ask, then, when expressions of anger well: "Am I building bridges that will lead to God?"

A closer look at the temple Jesus was clearing may help us move toward more insight about our own anger. The central location for building a relationship with God in first century Palestine was the Temple, the house of God.

This was the place where formal prayers were said in the name of the whole people, where the community came together to break bread and celebrate their life in God. The temple was the formal institution where people acknowledged the need for God in their lives.

It is easy to see that the Church has inherited the same central location today. . . as a clear sign to an unbelieving world that God wants a true relationship with His children.

However, since Christ has told us that the Kingdom of

God is within each of us, we know that this passage is about more than just buildings, whether it is "the temple" in first century Palestine, or "the Church" today. Christ was letting us know, in a very powerful way, that anger when it is expressed in ways that tear down obstacles to building authentic relating with God...both in self and others...is appropriate.

Anger can be constructive and build relationships with God and others, but it can also lead to destruction and alienation. An important first step in using anger to discover our true selves and build authentic relationships is to identify it. We need to be honest about our feelings. . . . it is healthy to simply recognize, "I am angry." If we don't identify what we are feeling honestly, attempting to avoid the anger welling up inside us by pushing it out of consciousness, we are only setting ourselves up for more pain.

Repressed anger is expressed indirectly: some people will turn the anger inwards on themselves instead of expressing it in a healthy way. Psychological studies have shown that this can lead to depression. It's like ingesting something toxic. Our internal world shuts down. The poisonous anger kills hope and so we feel depressed.

Some of us find dishonest ways of expressing our anger through passive-aggressive means such as always coming late to events involving people we are angry with, forgetting to do things we promised, or withholding words or deeds of love we know someone else is longing for.

Anger that is not identified can only lead us away from authentic relationship to God, which is our primary aim. Jesus identified the anger He felt about the way the traders were compromising and abusing authentic relating to God...and He drove them from the temple. What drove Him? A consuming passion for God, and His house.

After identifying honestly that we are angry, another

step is to try to find out what is driving our anger? Our immediate reaction is to say: "Of course I am angry when they treat me this way — anyone would be furious. . . ." But this is usually too simple an answer. Although some in similar circumstances seem untouched because they are just temperamentally milder, we know that there are others who are just as fiery as ourselves yet seem to be able to respond in more constructive ways to the same frustrations and circumstances we rage against. By constructive ways we don't mean that everything becomes nice and everyone loves us, but rather that there is less game playing and more sense of true identity as children of God.

To sort out helpful and unhelpful expressions of anger, we need to ask, "Is it a passion for God, and a desire to relate in an honest, Christ-like way, or has anger been building inside us from other situations; situations in which, for whatever reason, we did not express our anger honestly, and in a direct way that moved us toward authentic relating?"

For example, a woman feels pushed around by her boss. She conceals her anger for fear of losing her job, but then comes home and yells at the kids for being messy in an uncontrolled way, disproportionate to their "crimes." If we examine such behavior we realize that it involves a hypocritical stance of playing nice at work together with a habit of inappropriate explosions only at those who can't fight back. Psychologists call this displacement.

What would be a more Christian way to respond to a difficult boss? It is essential to begin with prayer, for this shows that we realize that no significant changes in our lives can come without God. After feeling sheltered in God's loving providence, we can begin to examine ways of balancing our emotional world.

Sometimes voicing a complaint in an objective non-sarcastic way can be a bridge to improved relations. If there is no satisfaction to be obtained by bringing about greater justice, we need to decide whether to "shake the dust" off our feet by quitting, or instead to offer the suffering of victimization to Christ as a penance. An honest confrontation of options, made in the security of prayer, can lead to more fair treatment of others around us who have nothing to do with the real problem.

Another way of understanding why we are so much more angry in some situations than in others is to ask this question: "Am I using my anger to protect injured parts of myself?" A blast of anger can be a way of getting others to back off. With this anger, I buy some space to regain some sense of security or power, "Don't tread on me or I'll hurt you worse than I hurt."

For instance, the boss may remind us of a parent who demeaned us. So, when the boss criticizes us, it opens the old wound of feeling inadequate: "Nothing I ever did was good enough. I'm not acceptable for who I am." Then, yelling at the kids puts me in the boss position. However nothing constructive comes out of it to build the Kingdom of God. Instead, we reinforce the old pattern of how a parental figure dominated over us and shamed us and we repeat this with our own children.

Breaking the pattern and living in our true selves begins by taking our feelings seriously. A counselor often interrupts a diatribe by asking: how did you feel when so and so treated you that way? Such a question connects the head and heart; the intellectual justification for anger with feelings of being demeaned, triggered by the situation. We say, "My boss is such a bully." The therapist asks: "What did you feel when he criticized you?"

If we are angry, we need to listen to the message our feelings are communicating to us. We *must* keep a *short* "account list." When the Scriptures advise us not to let the sun go down on our anger, it is telling us that holding on to anger and letting it build up inside us like a volcano ready to explode will not work. We must practice discernment, perceiving with God's help what is really involved in our anger. What connections can we make between the present feelings and another time we felt similarly? What was threatened in us?

In the case of the domineering boss, confrontation in a Christian spirit could take the form of setting up an interview in a conducive environment for mutual communication and talking about how we feel about patterns in our relationship. It is a sign of how close we are to Christ in prayer, and therefore how humble, that we can avoid accusatory defensive moves, instead making specific concrete suggestions that could lead to reconciliation and more direct communication.

## For Reflection

1. Are you afraid of your anger? What were messages about anger that you received growing up?

2. What are healthy ways you can process your anger, and keep a "short account list?"

3. What are some of the messages you need to hear your anger telling you about the ways you relate to self and others?

4. Are there particular times, places, or people that stir anger up inside you? Are there patterns that you need to identify and become more aware of? Is your anger a defense, a way of protecting injured parts of yourself? Is there a better way for you to relate to those wounds?

### *Guided Imagery*

Think of some recent example of someone or something that angered you greatly. As you think of it, form your hand into a fist.

Imagine yourself at the Temple in Jerusalem. You have just watched Jesus chasing the moneychangers away. You can still see the dust in the air and hear Jesus breathing deeply.

You approach Him and tell Him how angry you are. He listens intently. His face softens as you let it all out. His breathing becomes more and more even.

Look into His eyes and notice His concern for your feelings. See that He takes you seriously and cares about the injuries behind your expression of anger.

He reaches for your clenched fist offering His open hand. You feel the powerful yet gentle way He opens your hand one finger at a time.

As you look into His eyes you realize the truth that your life will always include injustices. This is a painful recognition but a step toward letting go, forgiving, and planning how you will confront those who are angering you.

# V
# John 3: 1 – 8 Jesus Teaches

## Nicodemus About Being Born Anew

### *The True Self, Free in the spirit*

And there was a man of the Pharisees, named Nicodemus, a ruler of the Jews.

This man came to Jesus by night and said to him: Rabbi, we know that thou art come a teacher from God; for no man can do these signs which thou dost, unless God be with him.

Jesus answered and said to him: Amen, amen, I say to thee, unless a man be born again, he cannot see the kingdom of God.

Nicodemus saith to him: How can a man be born when he is old? Can he enter a second time into his mother's womb and be born again?

Jesus answered: Amen, amen, I say to thee, unless a man be born again of water and the Holy Ghost, he cannot enter into the kingdom of God.

Unless a man be born again.

That which is born of the flesh is flesh: and that which is born of the Spirit is spirit.

Wonder not that I said to thee: You must be born again.

The Spirit breatheth where he will and thou hearest
his voice: but thou knowest not whence he cometh
and whither he goeth. So is every one that is born of
the Spirit.

(John 3: 1-8)

What does it mean to be "born again?" On a theological
level, to be "born again" means that we have made a decision to turn ourselves over to Jesus. . .that is, Christ becomes Lord over our lives.

On a psychological level being "born again" involves a
new relationship toward the issue of control. To make
Christ Lord of our lives fundamentally means that we are
no longer our own gods, and thus have "turned over the
reigns to God." We want Him henceforth to be the one in
control.

We are "born of the Spirit." This is most essentially
what it is to live in our true selves, the selves God made us
to be.

Perhaps an analogy might help explain how this can be
true. Imagine an ocean that is in a placid state. Someone
who always happened to go out to watch the sea at one
time of the day when there was a flat vista for miles ahead
might think that this was simply what an ocean was. Suddenly a powerful wind starts blowing over the waters. We
see huge waves pounding the shore. Which is the true
ocean? By analogy, the self we become when we are born
again in the Spirit is a manifestation of potentialities of
love of God and others we could not have imagined possible in our previous, more worldly state.

But, to become that new, freer, truer self means surrendering our previous sense of security, however illusory,
when our two feet were firmly planted on the earth with
most of our mental powers concentrated on how to cope
with daily problems.

On an intellectual level, "letting go and letting God" seems well and good. It makes good sense to turn control over to the loving God who is all-knowing, all-powerful, and always present for each one of us.

However, don't we all share a little in common with Nicodemus? The whole concept of being "born of the Spirit," on some level might feel just a little mysterious and anxiety provoking.

Jesus seems to pick up on this anxiety about spiritual existence, but His answer only seems to "fan the flames." "The wind blows where it wishes, and you can hear the sound of it, but cannot tell where it comes from or where it goes. So is everyone who is born of the Spirit."

There is a deep sense of freedom that comes with being "born of the Spirit," and thus discovering our true selves. St. Paul tells us that "where the Spirit of God is, the heart is free." Readers who think they have never really been born-again or surrendered their lives completely to Jesus might pause now and go to Him in prayer, begging Him to take them over.

Readers who do consider themselves to be born again may need to consider with us that the *amount* of freedom we enjoy after being "born again" is contingent on how much of our lives, our choices, our feelings, our hopes and fears, we continue to turn over to God. Even after an initial surrender, we can easily revert to "holding on" to parts of our lives. Fearful of giving up control, we choke off the freedom that comes with the presence of the Holy Spirit in our hearts.

"Control" is an illusion. Only God has control. Yet, many of us use the illusion of control to "cap" anxieties in our lives. The more chaotic we are feeling on the inside, the more we are going to *attempt* to control the outside. For some, the ideas just presented in this paragraph will be obvious. But for many others it will be rather new. You may be thinking right now: "Isn't this a little exaggerated? After all, I'm not just a wave blowing in the wind." Part of being human is to exercise free will in an effort to control external forces; for example, having a home alarm system or a retirement account. What really does it mean, then, to admit to not being in control? Let us examine a few test cases to understand control and surrender better in relationship to our true selves.

A storm is destroying all the homes in my beachfront town. After doing everything I can with sandbags to save it, I may find myself in a shelter, numb with the shock of having seen my house crumbling into the sea. If I am a person who thought that I was in control, my natural sense of loss may be compounded by severe desolation. I have defined myself as one who, through my sound management of finances, paid off my mortgage years ago and can now live contentedly, even on a small social security income. Now I will be truly poor since during the last storm the insurance company stopped covering houses in my area. Such a calamity can be devastating to one for whom "me" and "poor" are incompatible.

On the other hand, if my sense of who I am is simply a "child of God," in spite of some trauma, I can start up a new life as simply a poorer Christian whose fundamental identity has not changed. Because I have surrendered to God and given Him control, I can accept, after some struggle, sad circumstances as outwardly diminishing but inwardly acceptable.

Finding our life-styles changed for the worst is one test of our acceptance of God as Lord of our lives. Another test of who is in control can come from experiencing expanded ability. It may sound a little strange, but "possibility" can evoke deep anxiety. An example that readily comes to mind is that of a woman whose busy house has become an "empty nest" when all her children have left home. Others may envy her freedom, but she may feel lost and bewildered, with each day presenting so many possible choices of new activities to engage in. More personal freedom gets us in touch with a world full of possibilities. Of course, to pursue these possibilities and live in our true selves, we must live in freedom. This "stepping out in faith" means taking risks. For many, taking risks means opening ourselves up to failure, embarrassment, ridicule, and shame.

The truth is, though, that if we never experience personal freedom and take risks, we don't grow. . .we die a slow death from the inside out. Worst of all, to refuse to at least enter into the process of slowly giving up control of our lives to God will keep us from deep, personal relating to God. He will continue to seem distant, severe, and judgmental.

Let us listen to our anxieties. What are they trying to communicate to us about personal injuries and fears? It would be insensitive to pretend that this is an easy process — to give up control. The healing comes not in "heroic" acts of will but in understanding a given situation within a larger life context of hopes and fears. When the anxiety is severe enough to paralyze choice, it is a sign we need more community, perhaps supplemented by psychotherapy and spiritual direction. It may be helpful to become more connected to others, such as friends and relatives who accept us in love and are advocates for our true selves. It is imperative for us to understand that surrender to Jesus leads us out of isolation.

## For Reflection

1. In what ways are you "born again," that is, have you made a conscious choice to make Jesus Lord of your life?

2. What are your biggest issues of control — areas

where you feel you have to keep a tight hold on what is going on, or else suffer extreme anxiety? Are you at least in the process of letting go of control issues?

3. What does "letting go of control issues" mean to you? What does the process look like? Is there at least one other person who can support you in this difficult process?

4. Have you been able to identify certain fears you have, and the control mechanisms you choose in an attempt to cap the surface anxiety that accompanies the underlying fears?

5. What potentialities (relational and professional) are being stifled by a "fear to risk?"

### Guided Imagery

You are walking down a winding, hilly road. You carry a large sack. In it are all the aspects of your life you feel are in your own control. Picture each aspect, or item, as a brick.

Pause and list in your mind all those aspects of life you think you control such as projects, money, family members, people you give advice to. . . .

You see Jesus ahead, sitting beneath a tree smiling at you with an expression of gentle humor. He beckons you to sit next to him. . .then he asks you to give him each item in your sack.

You feel anxious. You ask "For keeps, or just for a few minutes?"

He responds "If you want your burden to be lighter, trust me."

You hesitate. What are you afraid of?

He does not pressure you. You have a sense that it is up to you to go on carrying the sack, or to surrender at least some of it.

You pick out one item to give to Jesus. Which one do

you choose?

You give it to Jesus. He holds it for a moment and when he gives it back you notice that it looks different.

Instead of being solid it is transparent. As you look through it you see not just the aspect of life you wanted to control but instead you see Jesus.

You feel peace knowing that ultimately he will bring about the greatest good for you in this area of your life, as you continue to share your anxieties with him moment by moment.

(You can repeat this exercise again with other areas of control.)

# VI

# John 4: 5 – 19, 39 Jesus Encounters the Samaritan Woman

## Overcoming Fear to Relate
## to the True Self of Others

He cometh therefore to a city of Samaria, which is called Sichar, near the land which Jacob gave to his son Joseph.

Now Jacob's well was there. Jesus therefore, being wearied with his journey, sat thus on the well. It was about the sixth hour.

There cometh a woman of Samaria, to draw water. Jesus saith to her: Give me to drink.

For his disciples were gone into the city to buy meats.

Then that Samaritan woman saith to him: How dost thou, being a Jew; ask of me to drink, who am a Samaritan woman? For the Jews do not communicate with the Samaritans.

Jesus answered and said to her: If thou didst know the gift of God and who he is that saith to thee: Give me to drink; thou perhaps wouldst have asked of him, and he would have given thee living water.

The woman saith to him: Sir, thou hast nothing wherein to draw, and the well is deep. From whence then hast thou living water?

Art thou greater than our father Jacob, who gave us the well and drank thereof, himself and his children and his cattle?

Jesus answered and said to her: Whosoever drinketh of this water shall thirst again: but he that shall drink of the water that I will give him shall not thirst for ever.

But the water that I will give him shall become in him a fountain of water, springing up into life everlasting.

The woman said to him: Sir, give me this water, that I may not thirst, nor come hither to draw.

Jesus saith to her: Go, call thy husband, and come hither.

The woman answered and said: I have no husband. Jesus said to her: Thou hast said well: I have no husband.

For thou hast had five husbands: and he whom thou now hast is not thy husband. This, thou hast said truly.

The woman saith to him: Sir, I perceive that thou art a prophet.

Now of that city many of the Samaritans believed in him, for the word of the woman giving testimony: He told me all things whatsoever I have done.

(John 4: 5-19,39)


Labels. They can be very helpful in communicating needs and wants. For instance, knowing that I have an "IBM" computer facilitates shopping for software. I can simply ask the salesperson to direct me towards the IBM compatible section. I'm off and running.

Or, when I know that someone was a Jew who lived through the Holocaust during World War II, I can be sure he will be especially sensitive to anti-Semitic threats in our days. Just hearing the two words "holocaust victim" is enough to make me particularly aware.

A third example might be the way we are using the term "true self" in this book to stand for the reality of "being all God made you to be."

There is so much information we take in on a daily basis that we need labels to help us receive, organize, and respond to incoming data. Yet, however useful labels can be, they can also destroy communication before it even begins and deeply injure people in the process. One may think of the frightened people in the Christian community who refuse to dialogue and learn from each other even in areas of agreement because, "she's Catholic" or "he's a charismatic." In bandying about such labels too facilely we can bury our true selves beneath characterizations that do not encompass all of who we are.

The passage in the Gospel of St. John about the Samaritan woman beautifully illustrates how to use labels as tools for processing without losing sight of the personal dimension. . .the feelings of the human beings involved.

Jesus has plenty of opportunities to play power games with the Samaritan woman. He is a "man," and she is a "woman". . . in first century Palestine, simple gender differences were often used to distance people from true relating. Sadly, there are many occasions in today's world where gender-biases still abuse, as in "don't even bother talking to him, he's a man, he won't understand."

Jesus moves past the gender distinction of his time which precluded a man speaking to a woman other than his family members, much to the Samaritan woman's surprise, and asks her for a drink.

Jesus was a "Jew" and the woman a "Samaritan." These two nations held deep-seated hatred for each other, yet Jesus sees their common humanity instead of a label.

Finally, Jesus speaks truthfully to the Samaritan woman about her relations with different men, without making a judgment in this context. Some might have responded to her answer that she was unmarried with a label like "adulterer," but the chance to relate, true self to true self, would have been lost. Feeling shame and perhaps anger, the woman would have buried her emotions and retreated from the perceived attacker.

Because Jesus had no false self but only a true self, he sought authentic relationship with the Samaritan woman. . .communication in Spirit and in truth. He refused to get stuck at the level of labels, and provided what she was so thirsty for, intimacy: first with God, and then with another human being. By feeling understood instead of judged, listened to instead of talked at, and accepted instead of shamed, the Samaritan woman was able to embrace her true self. . . the self God made her to be. . .and trust Jesus to be her Lord and Savior. She also shared the great gift of "everlasting water" with others. . .taking the risk and sharing her personal truth, revealed in Jesus.

How can our reflection about Jesus and the Samaritan woman bring us healing? Most importantly, we need to know deeply that Jesus does not see us, ourselves, in terms of labels such as successful or failing, attractive or ugly, Hispanic or Anglo. Sometimes when we "label" it is a defense mechanism to protect our own feelings of inferiority. When we let Jesus reach into our true selves, whom he judges to be infinitely valuable and lovable, then we can be kinder to others.

## For Reflection

1. What are some "labels" you are tempted to use in order to avoid true relating? Can you connect these labels, used to avoid communication, with internal fears you carry?

2. What does it mean to you to relate to someone "in spirit and in truth?" Can you connect this to a deeper un-

derstanding of your true self?

3. The Samaritan woman thirsted for intimate communication. . .relating on the level of spirit and truth. Can you identify a similar thirst in your own life for deep sharing? How have you tried to satisfy your thirst (maybe not all your efforts have proven helpful)?


### Guided Imagery

You come to the well where Jesus is drinking the water the Samaritan woman gave him. What does the well look like? Is it a warm day? Overcast? In a green field or in a desert place?

Just as you reach Jesus, you see someone you know well but dislike coming toward the well.

Jesus says: "tell me about that person who is coming." You respond with the worst label you use to characterize him or her.

When the "uninvited person" arrives, Jesus sits both of you down next to him and gives you each a drink of water.

What are you feeling now? Is there a fear that he will prefer the one you dislike? He suddenly faces you alone and he tells you something about the other person that surprises you. What is this insight? A fear or insecurity, perhaps a childhood wound? Suddenly you see the person you tend to label harshly as a frightened child.

Now think what label this person might place on you? What is Jesus showing them about the origin of your most difficult trait? Picture yourself as a little child. See Jesus with both you and the other person as little children. He is gently putting his arm around each of your shoulders. You see love and forgiveness in his eyes.

After he leaves what gesture do you want to make to the other person?

# VII
# John 5: 1- 15 Jesus Heals
# the Crippled Man

## Fear of Being Healed:
## an Impediment to the True Self

After these things was a festival day of the Jews: and Jesus went up to Jerusalem.

Now there is at Jerusalem a pond, called Probatica, which in Hebrew is named Bethsaida, having five porches.

Probatica. . . that is, the sheep pond; either so called, because the sheep were washed therein, that were to be offered up in sacrifice in the temple, or because it was near the sheep gate. That this was a pond where miracles were wrought is evident from the sacred text; and also that the water had no natural virtue to heal, as only one of those put in after the motion of the water was restored to health; for if the water had the healing quality, the others would have the like benefit, being put into it about the same time.

In these lay a great multitude of sick, of blind, of lame, of withered: waiting for the moving of the water.

And an angel of the Lord descended at certain times into the pond and the water was moved. And he that went down first into the pond after the motion of the water was made whole of whatsoever infirmity he lay under.

And there was a certain man there that had been eight and thirty years under his infirmity.

Him when Jesus had seen lying, and knew that he had been now a long time, he saith to him: Wilt thou be made whole?

The infirm man answered him: Sir, I have no man, when the water is troubled, to put me into the pond. For whilst I am coming, another goeth down before me.

Jesus saith to him: Arise, take up thy bed and walk.

And immediately the man was made whole: and he took up his bed and walked. And it was the sabbath that day.

The Jews therefore said to him that was healed: It is the sabbath. It is not lawful for thee to take up thy bed.

He answered them: He that made me whole, he said to me: Take up thy bed and walk.

They asked him therefore: Who is that man who said to thee: Take up thy bed and walk?

But he who was healed knew not who it was: for Jesus went aside from the multitude standing in the place.

Afterwards, Jesus findeth him in the temple and saith to him: Behold thou art made whole: sin no more, lest some worse thing happen to thee.

The man went his way and told the Jews that it was Jesus who had made him whole.

(John 5: 1-15)

"Do you want to be healed?" Oh, what an exquisite question. . .the crippled man had been lying by the pool of Bethsaida, suffering, for thirty-eight years, and Jesus moves immediately to the heart of the matter.

What did Jesus see in the eyes of this poor man, beaten down by years of despair and degradation? Did He see a malingerer, a crybaby manipulating other people through their emotions, a con man trying to milk the system? No, I believe our loving, compassionate Lord saw a broken man who longed for life but was terrified by the possibility that he might gain it. How like the crippled man we are!

Shackled by "duty," anxiety, and loss we settle for life as it is. Our existences become like straitjackets. What hope do we have that anything will ever be different, that we could actually experience the joy of our salvation. . . fullness of life in our true selves according to God's plan?

Here we must distinguish between bearing the burdens of our human lot, such as commuting long distances so that the family can live in a safe place, or nursing elderly relatives, and the deadness of spirit that comes when we try to deal with these crosses without hope and love. Heavy crosses are compatible with joy in the Spirit, but lives of quiet desperation are not.

What is the source of this all too facile resignation to deadness of spirit? Fear. Perhaps it is camouflaged by anger, resentment, even false-pride? One might recognize it in a ready-made excuse: "I could have done it if it wasn't for my boss," "I didn't get the right degree, or go to the right school, so how was I supposed to dream?" or even "I can't afford a true self, I've got a mortgage, a spouse, and three kids."

There are a million reasons why we should not begin growing into all that God made us to be, and each one of them is hatched in the den of Hell, and is grounded in fear. Although we could easily think that the crippled man was simply hopeless because there was no way for him to reach the healing waters, the implication of the passage is that this might have been some kind of excuse. But perfect love casts out fear. Jesus looked straight into the crippled man's eyes and asked him, "Do you want to be healed?"

So, what is the message about discovering the true self in this text? This may come as a shock, considering the immediacy of Christ's words and subsequent healing of the man, but I believe the message is in the process. The crippled man was suddenly able to walk. . .yet was this the conclusion of his search for his true self, or the beginning?

What are Christ's parting words? "Go, and sin no more." The Greek word for sin means "to miss the mark;" go, but don't miss the point of this miracle! The man could walk, but the journey of growing into his true self evidently was going to be on-going. Christ gives us the grace we need in spite of all failure and sin, repenting when we fall and calling on his mercy.

Awareness of the times when we miss the mark, such as giving way to uncontrolled, abusive anger or neglect of real needs of self or others, will slowly help us uncover patterns of fear that distort the truth. . .patterns that may have been present since childhood.

For example, a child receives the message that her feelings will not be taken seriously — you are not important, you don't count, do your chores, just behave and be quiet — so she represses the expression of loss and grief. Cut off from her feelings, now in the present after the death of a loved one, she finds herself responding to questions about how she is with neutral phrases such as "I'm fine." She neglects her own need for a time of tears and keeps going about her duties since her feelings don't count, but efficient performance of her work does count.

Accountability to a spiritual director and a psycho-therapist can be helpful for seeing the "forest from the trees," and can act as a safeguard against the illusion of self-sufficiency. "If even the death of beloved persons can't hurt me, nothing can. I am a rock, I am an island." A counselor can help us to see that taking such a stance can be a danger sign.

To return to the Gospel story, the crippled man had to take a step of faith first, before he could ever take a step with his legs. It was not a huge step; in fact it was a pretty conservative step to say the least. The man actually didn't even say yes, exactly. "Rise, take up your mat and walk." That was it. The man risked. He risked rising and falling down; he risked looking like a fool: he looked into the eyes of the Man who understands all our fears existentially and stepped in faith. . .and the journey of discovery had begun.

Discovering the true self is not a sudden revelation, although there will certainly be beautiful "showings" along the way. Discovery of the true self begins with small, tentative, baby steps of faith, and continues as we begin to sensitize ourselves to "missing the mark."

God doesn't expect us to conquer all our fears on our own, and then triumphantly answer, "Yes!" He simply encourages us gently to begin the long process of becoming who he made each one of us to be, through his Son Jesus. Begin the journey of discovering our true selves by looking into the eyes of Jesus and hearing him ask us, "Do you want to be healed?"

He's not asking you to be perfect, have all the answers, to feel only bright, happy feelings, but whether you want to begin the long journey of becoming your true self. And what of those crosses that never seem to be lifted? Here we must make heroic acts of trust that bearing those crosses will help us to become the person he wants us to be.

## For Reflection

1. Are there areas in your life that need healing? If so, how have you "covered" them up in the past?

2. Why would a person be tempted to answer, "No, I don't want to be healed."? Can you relate to a fear of "abundant life?"

3. In your own life, do you recognize patterns that have grown up around fear(s)?

4. Do you have a person (or people) that can gently help you understand why you "miss the mark" in being a true self?

5. Can you imagine what life would be like without fears? What would be different in your life?

### *Guided Imagery*

You are at the pool of Bethsaida. What is your un-healed area — physical or emotional? Christ approaches. In his eyes you see deep understanding and compassion. Identify a wound you wish could be immersed in healing waters. Can you remember some painful times in the past when this wound hurt you in an especially deep way?

Jesus does not pressure you, but he does offer help. What does he want you to understand about the whole picture? Is he telling you something about how your wound fits into the larger context of meaning in your life?

Does he hold you in his arms, take your hand, or simply sit beside you? Let him tell you what it will be like in eternity when you finally understand the place of your wound in the story of the salvation of your true self.

# VIII
# John 6: 41- 69 Jesus Announces the Eucharist

## Revealing the True Self
## in the Courage of Bold Utterance

The Jews therefore murmured at him, because he had said: I am the living bread which came down from heaven.

And they said: Is not this Jesus, the son of Joseph, whose father and mother we know? How then saith he: I came down from heaven?

Jesus therefore answered and said to them: Murmur not among yourselves.

No man can come to me, except the Father, who hath sent me, draw him. And I will raise him up in the last day.

Draw him. . . not by compulsion, nor by laying the free will under any necessity, but by the strong and sweet motions of his heavenly grace.

It is written in the prophets: And they shall all be taught of God. Every one that hath heard of the Father and hath learned cometh forth to me.

Not that any man hath seen the Father: but he who is of God, he hath seen the Father.

Amen, amen, I say unto you: He that believeth in me hath everlasting life.

I am the bread of life.

Your fathers did eat manna in the desert: and are dead.

This is the bread which cometh down from heaven: that if any man eat of it, he may not die.

I am the living bread which came down from heaven.

If any man eat of this bread, he shall live for ever: and the bread that I will give is my flesh, for the life of the world.

The Jews therefore strove among themselves, saying: How can this man give us his flesh to eat?

Then Jesus said to them: Amen, amen, I say unto you: except you eat the flesh of the Son of man and drink his blood, you shall not have life in you. Except you eat — and drink.

He that eateth my flesh and drinketh my blood hath everlasting life: and I will raise him up on the last day.

For my flesh is meat indeed: and my blood is drink indeed.

He that eateth my flesh and drinketh my blood abideth in me: and I in him.

As the living Father hath sent me and I live by the Father: so he that eateth me, the same also shall live by me.

This is the bread that came down from heaven. Not as your fathers did eat manna and are dead. He that eateth this bread shall live for ever.

These things he said, teaching in the synagogue, in Capharnaum.

Many therefore of his disciples, hearing it, said: This saying is hard; and who can hear it?

But Jesus, knowing in himself that his disciples murmured at this, said to them: Doth this scandalize you?

If then you shall see the Son of man ascend up where he was before?

If then you shall see.

And he said: Therefore did I say to you that no man can come to me, unless it be given him by my Father.

After this, many of his disciples went back and walked no more with him.

Then Jesus said to the twelve: Will you also go away?

And Simon Peter answered him: Lord, to whom shall we go? Thou hast the words of eternal life.

(John 6: 41-69)

The Bread of Life discourse is one of the most theologically significant passages in the New Testament. In it, Jesus reveals in profoundly personal terms who he is and a way he will be present to us for all ages.

However, it is not the theology that we want to focus on here in our search for the true self, but rather the reaction of the crowd and Jesus' subsequent response.

"In all truth I tell you, if you do not eat the flesh of the Son of man and drink his blood, you have no life in you."

Jesus speaks his truth. . .the truth of who he is, according to God's will. He knew that what he was teaching was difficult to understand, but he *never* wavered. And the response of the crowds following him? "After hearing it, many of his followers said, 'This is a hard saying. Who can listen to it?'"

Jesus recognized that what he had spoken would cost him. . . . Yet he does not apologize, he does not soften his message, he does not compromise who he is. In the face of rejection, he does not sacrifice his true self. He holds his ground. Something had to give. . .John 6: 67 tells us, "After this, many of his disciples went away and accompanied him no more."

Living in our true selves, and speaking our truth. . .the truth God gave us about who we are. . .can cost us a lot. We are all tempted to live our lives through other people's eyes. . .perform for the "audience" that surrounds us.

When we challenge ourselves not to "perform" for others, we do not mean to exalt the loner rebel. Of course there are times when we must perform in the sense of obedience to legitimate authority such as following the directives of a boss in a work situation. Even when an authority does not seem to be as wise as we are about a particular decision, God's will, certainly will often involve harmonizing our ideas with those of others.

Whereas obedience is grounded in love of God and holiness, what we call "performing" is grounded in fear and the desire to get the acceptance of others at any price. In effect, we enthrone them on God's throne.

Yet, being true to God and his will, out of the part of ourselves that has made a total commitment to him can be very difficult.

How hard it is to resist going along with a repulsive dirty joke or a racial slur, accepting it as part of life. How difficult it is to risk our jobs by objecting to some shady business practice. Or, to choose a quite different example, it could be hard for a person of a God-given, relaxed temperament to confess that he or she would prefer to watch the baseball game over engaging in a vehement political discussion the rest of the family wants to pursue.

In the short run, avoiding confrontation by means of pleasing, amiable behavior might buy us a false sense of security: "I have friends". . . "I'm popular". . ."I won't be abandoned." Oh, but at what cost. . .to live our lives through other's eyes will slowly destroy our true identities . . .the one-of-a-kind, special person God wants us to be.

And the farther we try to run from our true selves by performing for others, the more depressed we will become and the more angry we will feel. In the end, the fear of rejection, abandonment, or loss we tried desperately to avoid by being "everything to everybody" will come back to haunt us three times as fiercely. We may find that we hate to have lunch with others at work because we are tired of pretending to be just like them or the false image they are projecting. Clinging to the approval of parents, we may fail to enter the faith we are convinced is the true one.

We may be able to fool others for awhile. . .we may even be able to dupe ourselves for a brief period. However, as St. Augustine said, "God, you have made us for yourself. . .and our hearts are restless until they rest in thee."

And what is resting in God? It is being the person he made us to be. . .nothing more, nothing less. He doesn't ask us to perform; he simply asks us to be faithful. . .faithful to his plan for us. . .discovered as we live in our true selves guided by Holy Scripture and God's Church.

## For Reflection

1. What are some ways that you "live your life through other people's eyes"?

2. What are the fears that arise when you think about living in your true self, the self God made you to be? What do you think would happen if you stopped worrying about what others may think?

3. Can you feel the wounds behind the "performative self," the self that must be acceptable to everyone in the audience? What is the feared loss?

### *Guided Imagery*

Picture yourself in some role where you "perform" rather than acting out of the true self. If you are not sure what this means, measure your anxiety level in certain circumstances.

Picture yourself gritting your teeth or clenching your jaw while you play this role. You suddenly look up and see Jesus is watching you with sad eyes.

Stop and sit down next to Jesus. What does he tell you about how to change your way of living in order to be more your true self? When you see how to alter your attitudes or actions, either to leave the role, to modify it, or perform it in a different spirit, picture yourself with your new freedom of spirit.

Can you see Jesus smiling at you?

# IX
# John 8: 1 – 11 Jesus Confronts the Violent Judges of the Woman Taken in Adultery

## Finding True Relationship
## by Overcoming Harsh Judgment

And Jesus went unto Mount Olivet.

And early in the morning he came again into the temple: and all the people came to him. And sitting down he taught them.

And the Scribes and Pharisees brought unto him a woman taken in adultery: and they set her in the midst,

And said to him: Master, this woman was even now taken in adultery.

Now Moses in the law commanded us to stone such a one. But what sayest thou?

And this they said tempting him, that they might accuse him. But Jesus bowing himself down, wrote with his finger on the ground.

When therefore they continued asking him, he lifted up himself and said to them: He that is without sin among you, let him first cast a stone at her.

And again stooping down, he wrote on the ground.

But they hearing this, went out one by one, beginning at the eldest. And Jesus alone remained, and the

woman standing in the midst.
Then Jesus lifting up himself, said to her: Woman,
where are they that accused thee? Hath no man con-
demned thee?
She said: "No man, Lord." And Jesus said: "Neither
will I condemn thee. Go, and now sin no more."

(John 8: 1- 11)

There are two worlds that are superimposed on each other:
the world of love and the world of fear. Each day, in a
myriad of different ways, God gives us the choice of
which world we want to live in.

The passage of the woman caught in the act of adultery
provides a wonderful example of the two worlds collid-
ing. Jesus, who resides at the heart of the world of love, is
confronted in the temple area by the world of fear, repre-
sented by the terrified woman and the Scribes and Pharisees. We know from the context of the Scriptures that
these men did not have loving intentions in mind. They
not only intended to stone the woman, they were hoping
to get Jesus to say something that they could charge him
with.

Of course, Jesus saw through their "law of Moses"
smoke-screen to their inflated egos and their hypocrisy,
and decided to teach them about the world of love. He began by re-focusing the issue at hand, moving from the
woman's sin to their condemning attitudes.

Does this mean that sin is inconsequential? Absolutely
not. Sin is serious, and destructive, and separates us from
God and from our true selves. Christ's last words to the
woman were, "Go, and sin no more."

The difference between the two worlds is found in the
question of purpose. Those who live in the world of love
are fundamentally committed to healing and wholeness. . .
to a process of becoming a true self. They see that

people's lives are transformed by grace and forgiveness, and a deep realization that they are loved not for what they do or don't do, but rather for who they are as children of a loving God.

When we live in the world of fear we avoid confrontation with the true selves of others. We want to stay in a position where we can point fingers, and criticize, and act holy. We make ourselves judge and jury, and convict people who fall short of perfection. Our goal is to control everyone around us through fear, shame, and guilt. If anyone "steps out of line," we are there to bring the hammer down.

When we act this way, we are in denial; denial of our sinfulness, denial of our own need for forgiveness, denial of our dependence on God's grace to make it through another day. We live in the illusion that we have all the answers, and hide behind rules and regulations. We believe that as long as we can stay busy condemning others, we can avoid our own glaring issues. . .our own massive fears, building within.

Clearly the woman caught in the act of adultery frightened the Scribes and Pharisees. She was a mirror. In her brokenness and humanness she reminded these self-righteous men that they were broken and human. On some level of consciousness, they must have recognized that they, too, were capable of adultery as well as any number of other sins. . .and this was unacceptable. (Some commentators believe that Jesus was writing on the ground the names of sins of each of the accusers.) They could not afford to look at the truth; they had lived too long in their false selves, projecting an image of invulnerability to sinful temptations.

So, the inhabitants of the world of fear wanted to stamp out this woman caught in the act of adultery. But Jesus insured that love would carry the day. The sinless Savior of the world refused to condemn. He was merciful and loving and totally committed to transformation and the true self.

### Guided Imagery

You are holding a stone in your hand.

Who do you want to throw it at?

Jesus takes Your hand and asks if you are willing to let the stone fall? If you say yes, Jesus opens your fingers and sets the stone aside.

He asks you why the person you want to throw a stone at frightens you. Because this person's sin manifests your own secret temptation? Because you think he or she could mortally wound you?

Jesus gently reminds you that he is in charge. He will give you strength to resist temptation or to survive any attack however unfair because he understands what it means to be hated by the World. How do you feel as you hear his words?

Now he turns to the person you were going to stone to tell him or her to go and sin no more.

# X

# John 9–, 1 – 3 Jesus Heals the Blind Man

## The True Self Develops
## in Acceptance of our Crosses

And Jesus passing by, saw a man who was blind
from his *birth.*

And his disciples asked him: Rabbi, who hath
sinned, this man or his parents, that he should be
born blind?

Jesus answered: Neither hath this man sinned, nor
his parents; but that the works of God should be
made manifest in him.

(John 9: 1-3)

There is something in the human spirit that wants to have
all of life's mysteries solved. "Loose ends" seem to gnaw
at us. If there are unanswered questions, then the world is
not the predictable place we have imagined it to be. We
are confronted with the realization that we don't have
nearly the control over events and people that we as-
sumed.

Living life in the true self must include a respect for
the dimension of mystery. . .that not everything is explain-
able this side of Heaven. Wholeness and balance are ef-

fected as we look for insights rather than "answers," and slowly learn to love the questions.

This does not mean a passive giving up on initiative to simply wait for God to do everything without our cooperation, as irresponsible people sometimes do. But if we really trust in God's Providence, do we need to know what we will be doing ten years from now? "'There is hope for your future,' says the Lord." (Jeremiah 31: 17)

In the passage about the man born blind, the disciples ask Jesus who was to blame for the man's blindness. Blame is often used to avoid confrontation with the dimension of mystery. Blame gives us a cause and effect relationship that explains "why." If I do this, then this will happen. Everything seems neat and tidy. . .so understandable.

Here are two examples of the way some people try to assign blame to avoid the mysterious dimension of undesirable circumstances of life:

"Anyone could tell you why you got cancer of the throat! You use a microwave and its just level with your neck!"

"I told you your marriage would break up if you confronted your wife directly about your feelings."

Even if someday it is shown that microwaves cause cancer or that sometimes direct confrontation leads to divorce, the blame is probably somewhat unreasonable. After all, cancer existed way before microwaves and many marriages flourish because husbands and wives talk things out.

Living in the true self must include a respect for, and a contentment with, the dimension of mystery, the unfathomable, precisely because God is mystery. . .his ways are unsearchable. . .no one knows his mind.

The true self accepts this, and trusts more and more in God's faithfulness and loving kindness. How much more secure we feel when, through closeness to God in sacraments and prayer we recognize that he himself will be there for us and that we don't have to try to control realities and persons around us.

The false self wants to hold onto control, and attempts to fit everything and everyone into cubbyholes. Only then can one feel safe. . ."no arrows in the night," no sneak attacks. To use a common example of a usually fruitless attempt to try to control the future, consider employees during lunch breaks sitting around the cafeteria trying to find an angle on the boss. They imagine that if they scrutinize his or her behavior and character long enough they will discover ways they can manipulate him or her, and guarantee the safety of their jobs. Then they can feel safe. Or can they? Instead of getting long term contracts they may all lose their jobs because of unpredictable factors having nothing to do with the manager, such as economic realities in a soft market. In fact, there will always be factors we cannot predict.

The compulsive desire for predictability robs people of "sacramental sensibility," an awareness of God's loving presence surrounding us daily. Those engaging in gossipy talk over lunch about office politics may fail to really show sympathy for a friend at work whose father just died. They may make half-hearted gestures, but they are too busy strategizing to really care about what is so much deeper in their own lives and those of their co-workers.

How do we meet God in the experience of job insecurity? Some constantly question God, asking: "How could you let hard workers suffer from unemployment?"

It's not wrong to question God. The Psalmist does it all the time. But we must heed his example of listening for God's response, recognizing that it might not be what we want to hear. In our fear of being fired, we might not be open to hear Jesus saying "I want you to find security in me and not in your job," or "I want you to become more compassionate to the poor by understanding their plight from within."

Fearing the mystery that could include deeper reasons for suffering than we want to hear is, in essence, telling God that you really don't trust that he is sovereign. . .telling God that perhaps he can't handle the universe, and that good may not prevail over evil after all.

When the false self (the one that believes that we can handle everything ourselves) rejects mystery, reductionism is bound to follow. God's universe gets shrunk down to what can be measured and predicted. Science and statistics give the only explanations that count.

So, when Jesus provides the answer about the cure of the blind man, "neither he nor his parents sinned; it is so that the works of God might be made manifest in him," this cause is neither physical nor inter-generational but purely spiritual and therefore outside of human control.

God's ways are not our ways, his ways are perfect. Little St. Therese wrote that all is grace because it comes from God. What is asked of us, in accepting this teaching, and embracing the dimension of mystery? Does it mean that we should stop studying, stop analyzing, and stop yearning for answers and alleviation of the pain in the world?

No. God gave us minds to probe the questions that appear before us. . .curiosity to "flavor" life with. The issue is one of purpose. Is our search aimed towards knowing God, and growing in relationship with him, or is it to avoid God and life in the Spirit? Are we attempting to surrender more and more to Divine Providence, or control the people and circumstances we come in contact with?

# For Reflection

1. How is the true self nurtured by "loving the questions?" What does loving the questions mean to you?

2. What does the dimension of mystery mean to you? Does the reality of mystery frighten you on some level? Why?

3. Can you think of ways that the true self can actually be avoided by misusing "mystery?" How can this be guarded against?

### Guided Imagery

Think of part of the future you are anxious about. You go to visit Mother Mary for advice. You tell her you can't understand why you have to go through so much uncertainty.

Mary asks you if you are angry at God. She also asks you what you are afraid of? She invites you to tell her about these fears and about people whose judgments frightened you in the past.

Mary takes your hands and tears fill her eyes. You know she understands, as you remember her fears of judgment about being a pregnant, unwed mother.

She asks you to pray the Our Father with her, placing your future in the hands of the God of Love.

As you get up to leave, Mary touches the side of your face. Even though there are no easy answers about the concrete steps to future goals, she promises to be with you. You feel new hope and trust.

# XI
# John 11: 32 – 35 The Raising of Lazarus

## Discovering the Eternity of
## the True Self as We Mourn Losses

When Mary therefore was come where Jesus was, seeing him, she fell down at his feet and saith to him. Lord, if *thou hadst been here, my brother had not died.*
Jesus, therefore, when he saw her weeping, and the Jews that were come with her weeping, groaned in the spirit and troubled himself,
And said: Where have you laid him? They say to him: Lord, come and see.
And Jesus wept.

(John 11:32-35)

How difficult it is to mourn a loss. Mourning asks us, in truth, to look at what was and what will never be. On a deep level, mourning reminds us that we live in a world that is predominantly temporal in nature. St. Paul says that what is visible will pass away.

We put so much trust in the visible. . .in youth, in physical strength, in material wealth. We are often shocked to hear that a man in his early fifties has died of a heart attack, or a wealthy business person has gone bank-rupt, or a beautiful home has burned to the ground.

The temptation is to try and avoid the process of mourning. . .to find a rational reason for why the "unex-pected" occurs: well, he smoked too much; she was under-insured; the house didn't have enough smoke alarms.

The truth is that life is fragile and the things of this world will pass away. If we don't grasp this fact, and be-gin to mourn that which we have lost, then we can never let the loss go. We become trapped by the pain that we keep trying to repress. We never move through the tempo-ral mourning to the eternal joy.

Many of us don't realize we are refusing to mourn be-cause we imagine it is better to hold ourselves together, lest we never stop crying, or we think others will admire us for not missing a day of work. . .or we want to impress God and others with our un-real "holy" resignation.

Our passage in the eleventh chapter of John speaks beautifully to the process of mourning and letting go. Jesus was not unmoved by the passing of his friend Lazarus, and the sorrow of those who loved him. When Christ saw Mary the sister of Lazarus crying, the Scrip-tures tell us that he was deeply troubled, and going to see the body he wept. Yes, the Son of God, the second Person of the Blessed Trinity wept at the loss. Jesus knew that he was going to raise Lazarus from the dead, and one may wonder why he would weep. . .everything was gong to be all right, wasn't it?

There was already loss involved. . .pain was already being experienced by the loved ones of Lazarus. . .and Christ, full of compassion, refused to deny the reality that in this life pain is unavoidable. Jesus shows that to live in our true selves means that we must be emotionally present in this world; we must be willing to weep with those who weep. And when we lose someone or something that matters to us, we must be willing to mourn the loss and feel the pain. . .not because we are depressive types, but because we must feel the sorrow if we are truly going to feel the joy. We must look at the loss, acknowledge it, before we can let it go.

So how does mourning help us let go of the loss, and the pain that accompanies it? It peels back layers of defenses that have been in place, guarding against feeling emotions that are uncomfortable. As we mourn losses, we live in the uncertainty of anxiety about letting go and trusting God. We learn to more fully live in reality.

We think we will never laugh or love again. Slowly, we see that loss is only a door leading to a deeper level of existence; not because grief is an illusion, but because God is Love, and has declared that life will carry the day. For instance, the lovableness of the missed person could never have been there unless there was a God who created him or her with such interior beauty of soul.

Since we detected that goodness in the other surviving so many bodily changes — from young to old, from brunette to gray-haired, from tiny baby to mature adult, we are the ones who can most affirm our conviction that the spirit of a human being is made to survive bodily changes even bodily death, as philosophers prove and Christ promises. (For more about immortality and eternal life see Ronda Chervin, *Victory Over Death*, St. Bede's Press).

Mourning takes us to the very center of the Christian message; we live in a dying and rising universe. . .dying because of sin, rising because of the atoning work of Jesus on Calvary. By dying, Christ destroyed the power of death and of any loss; by rising Christ restored our lives. . .He gives us a way out of the despair of loss. Loss does not have to have the final word. Follow the way of the risen Lord. . .mourn and feel what needs to be felt, recognizing that in the life of faith we must walk through Good Friday in order to arrive at Easter Sunday.

## For Reflection

1. List the losses in your life that readily come to mind.

2. Have you given yourself the time and space needed to really mourn these losses. . .felt what needed to be felt?

3. Are you aware of losses that you are not dealing with? Do you have a sense of why it is difficult to mourn these losses? What is gained, or avoided, by "hanging on" to that which will never be?

4. Do you have a community that can facilitate this mourning process? Is it difficult to "let down" around other people?

### *Guided Imagery*

Picture one person you have lost. You are holding onto the hand of this beloved person. You realize you have to let go. You see him or her receding from your vision.

You feel great grief. Then you begin to see a cloud of witnesses: Jesus, angels, saints, Mary and others who have gone before. They all reach out their hands and bring your loved one into the cloud . . . .

Now the cloud itself recedes. You notice that you are enveloped in the light of the Holy Spirit and there is a peace that passes all understanding as you see the cloud ascend. You know that the Comforter is with you just as Jesus promised. You are not alone and your loved one is present with you though you cannot understand how.

## XII
# John 12: 24 – 27 The Parable of the Grain of Wheat

## Dying of the Ego to Give Life to the True Self

Amen, amen, I say to you, unless the grain of wheat
falling into the ground die,
Itself remaineth alone. But if it die it bringeth forth
much fruit. He that loveth his life shall lose it and he
that hateth his life in this world keepeth it unto life
eternal.
If any man minister to me, let him follow me: and
where I am, there also shall my minister be. If any
man minister to me, him will my Father honour.
Now is my soul troubled. And what shall I say? Father, save me from this hour. But for this cause I
came unto this hour.

(John 12: 24-27)

In the search for your true selves, it is crucial to make the
distinction between ego-hood and personhood. Ego-hood
is expressed through rugged individualism, in the spirit of
"God helps those who help themselves." Personhood is
seen in authentic community, where one loves God with
everything, with our whole hearts, and loves the neighbor
as self.

Ego-hood insists that "it's a dog-eat-dog world, and only the fit survive." Personhood recognizes that relationships grounded in Love are worth sacrificing for, and "survival" is found in dying. Survival is found in dying? That is what Jesus tells us: ". . . unless a grain of wheat falls to the ground and dies, it remains alone; but if it dies, it produces much fruit." He is not only speaking of his own death on Calvary, he is providing us with an insight into the search for the true self.

The prophetic language of "dying" can be problematic. Well-intentioned people have misunderstood Christ's call to "hate" one's life in this world. They have gone out in search of suffering in such a way as to forget the joy of their salvation. They have made a cult of pain and misery, and neglected to accept the abundant life in Christ. We are not referring here to Christians who feel called to choose heroic suffering for the kingdom. We are questioning, instead, choices such as a person isolating himself or herself under the guise of needing to suffer alone, to fight demons in the desert. Or, suppose I am depressed, a friend offers to take me out to dinner. I say "No, I am fasting." But Jesus suggests that those who fast should manifest joy, washing their faces with oil. If, in fact, the pleasure of a good meal and good company could bring me out of my sad state of mind, it would be wrong to proudly disdain the offer on the basis that suffering is good for the soul. I need to admit that I need some recreation.

So, when Jesus tells us to die to ourselves, he does not mean we should omit all joy from our lives. What he is saying is that we must risk the "death" of giving over our own will for the sake of the ultimate joy he can give us.

The path of the true self, the path God has ordained for each one of us, may well have its particular trials and tribulations. We must not shudder to enter into close relationships or commitments such as marriage because we are afraid of the pain of being hurt, or the burden of child-raising. If we flee from love in fear we will lose out on the joys of true understanding or the delights of family life. A man or woman who chooses to be single for the Lord or to be a consecrated celibate priest, brother or sister, is not choosing to die to relationship, but rather to physical expression of intimacy in order to be closer to God and to others in a spiritual bond.

St. Paul reminds us that we share in Christ's sufferings so that we can share in his glory. Jesus is realistic about this: "I am troubled now. Yet what should I say? Father, save me from this hour?" Jesus shows us that God's will never takes us where his grace cannot sustain us. He remains faithful to us, and never abandons us.

The message Christ imparts to all of us who seek our true selves is to die to ego-hood; die to our non-relational, self-centered agendas for personal gratification and success and insulation from all problems. An example might be all those times when some of us feel tempted to retreat from others into workaholism, to shut out the real need for dialogue with close friends and family members.

The true self and true happiness is found when we die to that which is false. . .slowly letting go of control and fear, and illusions of self-sufficiency. . .allowing ourselves to be born again into personhood, willing to enter into the crucible of authentic relating, transformed by God's grace in the Body of Christ.

In Christ we truly become successful and productive, for the fruit we bear is purified by the Spirit and becomes eternally significant.

## For Reflection

1. In your own life can you envision what ego-hood has looked like? And what personhood has looked like?

2. As you reflect on the "dying," Christ may be asking of you, what are the feelings that emerge? Do you have a sense of issues or people for whom you need to suffer?

3. What are the issues of control that are attached to these situations? Ways that you try to force things to happen unnaturally, to "fix" things according to your terms and not God's?

4. How do you see yourself bearing your cross (there may be more than one)? Do you have a community that can help encourage you as you give of yourself, carrying those crosses?

### *Guided Imagery*

You are walking in a field of wheat. The wind is blowing. You see golden waves of swaying wheat. The Resurrected Jesus approaches smiling. You feel peace. He plucks a strand of wheat and squeezes it in his hand. As he reaches you he opens his hand. You see the seeds falling from the stalk, and you see the nail mark in the palm of his hand.

He asks you if you understand that there are different seasons in life, and even in the midst of winter you can find an eternal summer in the love which has urged you on to sacrifice in obedience to his will.

You see in his face that he knows how hard the sacrifice is for you. He asks you if you are willing to continue to carry your cross with him at least a while longer?

How do you respond to your Savior's call?

# XIII

# John 13: 1 – 17 Jesus Washes the Feet of the Apostles

## Loving Service from the True Self

Before the festival day of the pasch, Jesus knowing that his hour was come, that he should pass out of this world to the Father: having loved his own who were in the world, he loved them unto the end.

Before the festival day of the pasch and when supper was done (the devil having now put into the heart of Judas Iscariot, the son of Simon, to betray him),

Knowing that the Father had given him all things into his hands and that he came from God and goeth to God,

He riseth from supper and layeth aside his garments and, having taken a towel, girded himself.

After that, he putteth water into a basin and began to wash the feet of the disciples and to wipe them with the towel wherewith he was girded.

He cometh therefore to Simon Peter. And Peter saith to him: Lord, dost thou wash my feet?

Jesus answered and said to him: What I do, thou knowest not now; but thou shalt know hereafter.

Peter saith to him: Thou shalt never wash my feet, Jesus answered him: If I wash thee not, thou shalt have no part with me.

Simon Peter saith to him: Lord, not only my feet, but also my hands and my head.

Jesus saith to him: He that is washed needeth not but to wash his feet, but is clean wholly. And you are clean, but not all.

For he knew who he was that would betray him; therefore he said: You are not all clean.

Then after he had washed their feet and taken his garments, being set down again, he said to them: Know you what I have done to you?

You call me Master and Lord. And you say well: for so I am.

If then I being your Lord and Master, have washed your feet; you also ought to wash one another's feet.

For I have given you an example, that as I have done to you, so you do also.

Amen, amen, I say to you: The servant is not greater than his lord: neither is the apostle greater than he that sent him.

If you know these things, you shall be blessed if you do them.

(John 13: 1-17)

What an unforgettable scene; Jesus, the Word of God Incarnate, washing the feet of his disciples. This beautiful narrative provides us with deep insight into the quest for the true self. We, as Christians, are called to serve others. It is critical to the discovery of our true selves, and to our very faith. Jesus tells us in this passage to do as he has done.

But is service alone what Jesus models for us in washing the feet of the disciples? A key element to understanding what Jesus lives out for us in this passage is found in the second half of the first verse: "He loved his own in the world and he loved them to the end."

What does this mean? Jesus served his disciples because he loved them. He did not serve them because he had to; there was no compulsive nature to his love. He was not trying to earn their respect, or their loyalty. His actions were grounded in love. This sounds so simple, but how many of us can honestly say that we act out of love?

Here is a clear distinction between the true self and the false self: the final cause of action for the true self is love. . .the final cause of action for the false self is fear. Ultimately the true self acts for God, and the false self "performs" for the approval or acceptance of people, while forgetting God.

There is no judgment or condemnation intended here, for we all struggle not to act out of fear. Fears of abandonment, loss, and rejection are bound to haunt all of our lives at one time or another. So how can we move toward our true selves, living acts of charity?

From a psychological vantage point, two concepts emerge: boundaries and limits. Simply put, boundaries are an understanding of how far one can extend oneself, and limits are an understanding of how far one will let other people push. It is necessary that we have a sense of our internal worlds if we hope to recognize boundaries and limits. Feelings can act as valuable "guides," especially as we ask the Holy Spirit to "lead us into all truth."

How does this all work together? Here's an example: A man walks in the door from a hard day at work, dead tired, and his daughter asks him for help with her homework. The man feels angry inside. His boundaries and limits have been pushed all day at work: undo pressure from his boss to finish a report; clients stand him up for a business lunch and his car door is scratched in the parking lot. The anger he feels, and listens to, gives him a clear sense that he has had a tough day and needs to take a few minutes to unwind, perhaps with a walk around the block, before helping his daughter.

In the past, he has bent to guilt feelings, fearing that his daughter would not feel he was a good dad if he said "no" or "not right now." However, the Spirit of God has shown him that it is O.K. to admit that he has needs. Another day he may feel like helping immediately, without any hint of anger or resentment, but for tonight he needs a little break first. Often, just five or ten minutes of freedom from demands is all one needs to feel refreshed! Remember, Sabbath is a gift from God. . .a time to rest in His love.

Some may feel all this talk about personal needs is selfish. However, Jesus tells us to love God first, and then love neighbor as self. There is a healthy balance and equality implied here between our needs and our neighbor's, grounded in our love for God.

If a lighthouse remains lit, without any consideration of fuel, its light will eventually go out, and disasters will follow! We are the same in that if we serve without any sense of our boundaries and limits, we will not know if we are acting out of love or out of our false selves, "performing" for others instead of serving God. We must listen to what we are feeling, and ask the Holy Spirit to help us interpret the messages our feelings are giving us. Only then can we begin to approach the service, grounded in love, that Jesus models for us in washing the disciples' feet.

## For Reflection

1. Do you feel as if you understand the concepts of boundaries and limits in your own life? A clarifying question is: Do I feel free to say "no" or "not right now"?

2. What has your history of boundary and limit setting been? Is it hard for you to rest and claim Sabbath time?

3. How do you "play" (e.g. hobbies, interests, activities that are life-giving for you?) Do you make it a point to

find time to play? Do you see the connection in your own life between constructive, planned play/recreation and feeling restored and ready to serve in love?

### *Guided Imagery*

Picture yourself doing a task you tend to do in a frantic, compulsive manner, making unnecessary deadlines for yourself with tyrannical urgency.

Suddenly you see Jesus nearby watching you with gentle amusement. He says, "If you're not too busy, I'd like a little time out with you."

You hesitate. An inner voice says: "No. I have to finish what I started first." What do you feel when you think of letting it go?

You laugh and let him lead you out for a walk.

After a little while you hear him tell you that you don't have to earn his love by performing — by finishing everything quickly and perfectly. He tells you:

"I want to give you the desires of your heart — bring you what my Father has stored up for you since the beginning of time. Won't you give me more time to be with you?

Let me give you the peace and reassurance to do everything you do in serenity for me."

# XIV
# John 15: 1 – 4 The Parable of Pruning

## Discipline Reveals the Beauty of the True Self

I am the true vine: and my Father is the husbandman.
Every branch in me that beareth not fruit, he will
take away: and every one that beareth fruit, he will
purge it, that it may bring forth more fruit.
Now you are clean, by reason of the word which I
have spoken to you.
Abide in me: and I in you. As the branch cannot bear
fruit of itself, unless it abide in the vine, so neither
can you, unless you abide in me.

(John 15: 1-4)

We live in an age where a "disciplined life" is often seen
as rigid, oppressive, and generally unattractive. This passage speaks of the nature of a disciplined life in Christ,
and on the surface may not appear very inviting. Yet
Christ tells us that this is the way to a deeper relationship
with God, and a fruitful existence in our true selves. The
key to understanding discipline in Christ, which is ultimately life-giving, is in recognizing the means God uses
to tend and prune his own.

Could these be examples of such pruning? A Christian
woman is hoping to be married someday. In the meantime

the men she dates pressure her for sex before marriage. It is hard to trust enough in Christ to take a chance of losing potential husbands by insisting on following Christ's law of chastity. A man thinks he has a vocation to the priesthood. The vocation director tells him he must first pay off his debts before entering the seminary. But this may take several years. He has to trust that accepting the injunctions of the vocation's director is the will of Christ.

God forms us by means of his Son's commandments, commandments of love. He does not shame us or degrade us when we fall short of our true selves, but rather he reminds us that we must love him first and then love neighbor as self. It is there that the disciplined life becomes so important, for try as we may we will find loving in a Christ-like manner to be incredibly difficult. The woman seeking a husband may find loving Christ first instead of trying to hold onto a man through sex incredibly difficult. The future seminarian may find himself tempted to evade the love of neighbor involved in paying off debts to satisfy justice. He may want, instead, to carry on an inner dialogue where he berates Church authority for being so "petty" as to make such demands on him.

We are fallen in nature, and sin continues to serve as an obstacle to our journeys toward wholeness. The disciplined life is like the guard rail on the freeway, there to remind us that we need to stay on a straight path. By the very fact that spiritual disciplines are needed, just like guard rails, it is clear that we all wander from time to time. We must lean on God's grace in order to love, free from selfish motives.

The disciplined life in Christ, revealed throughout the Gospels, is grounded in the Holy Spirit. Our works are fruits of the Spirit, and it is the Spirit that leads us into all truth. There are three hallmarks to a disciplined life which might serve to direct us on our journey: dedication to prayer, obedience to the revealed truths of the Holy Scripture and Sacred Tradition, and accountability to a community grounded in Jesus Christ.

Along with prayer, we must be obedient to the Scripture and to the teachings of Christ's Church, led by the Holy Spirit. We cannot form ourselves, and it was not God's intention for us to try to be whole outside of the Body of Christ. The higher we climb on our spiritual journey the higher Satan climbs and if we lean on our own understanding, we are setting ourselves up for disaster. We must humbly submit to God's plan for holiness, revealed in his Word and in his Church. (If you have difficulty with any particular moral teaching of the Church you might consult Ronda Chervin's book *Living in Love,* St. Paul's Books and Media)

Finally, we cannot allow ourselves to become isolated from spiritual community. It might be tempting, at times, to consider ourselves as self-sufficient, but not even Jesus tried to live life without a community. He *began* by choosing his twelve apostles, to bond with and share life with. The spiritual community we choose to be intimate with, needs to be one that is committed to the truth of Jesus Christ, and led by the Holy Spirit. Great discernment and prayer should go into our choices regarding community, for they will share an important role in our disciplined life! A disciplined life in Christ can feel like pruning at times, but it is this tending by our heavenly Father that will keep us in the vine, Jesus, safe from serious and even eternal harm. . .and full of love.

## For Reflection

1. What do you think of when you hear the word "discipline?" Can you see how earthly and heavenly discipline might be similar, and how they might differ?

2. Have you felt "pruned" by God recently? Can you recall how you responded at the time, and how you feel about it now?

3. Do you practice spiritual disciplines in your life such as the hallmarks listed above? Are you in a formal formation program with a spiritual director and/or a spiritual community? If so, how has that experience been for you? If not, might you seek such helps?

4. What are some of the dangers of becoming isolated in your spiritual journey toward your true self?

### *Guided Imagery*

You are in the backyard of your dwelling. It is full of weeds and tangled branches. The sunlight cannot get through. The grass is brown. The air is heavy with decay and mildew. There is no freshness or new growth because everything has grown wild and of its own accord, without any sense of design or landscaping plan.

You see an ad stuck in the jamb of your door from a gardener. Your first thought is: "No, no, no. They'll just make it like all the other gardens on this block — stiff and stylized, everything in perfect rows — nothing spontaneous and free."

Now picture St. Joseph coming to visit. He asks to see your garden. You feel embarrassed. He looks out the window and instead of scolding you he says: "This is a wonderful plot of land you have with a lot of potential. Would you let me work with you on the design? I can prune your branches and let some of the sunlight shine through."

You let St. Joseph be your gardener. After all the work is done, you invite him to supper.

After he leaves, you lie awake listening to the wind rustling through your garden. You wonder where your own personal life might benefit from some pruning also.

# XV
# John 21:15 – 19 Jesus Asks
# if Peter Loves Him

## The True Self Flourishes in Gentle Loving

When therefore they had dined, Jesus saith to Simon Peter: Simon, son of John, lovest thou me more than these? He saith to him: Yea, Lord, thou knowest that I love thee. He saith to him: Feed my lambs.

He saith to him again: Simon, son of John, lovest thou me? He saith to him: yea, Lord, thou knowest that I love thee. He saith to him: Feed my lambs.

He said to him the third time: Simon, son of John, lovest thou me? Peter was grieved because he had said to him the third time: Lovest thou me? And he said to him: Lord, thou knowest all things: thou knowest that I love thee. He said to him: Feed my sheep.

Amen, amen, I say to thee, When thou wast younger, thou didst gird thyself and didst walk where thou wouldst. But when thou shalt be old, thou shalt stretch forth thy hands, and another shall gird thee and lead thee whither thou wouldst not.

And this he said, signifying by what death he should glorify God. And when he had said this, he saith to him: Follow me.

(John 21: 15-19)

83

Living in our true selves is an on-going challenge, and its appropriate to end our journey through the Gospel of St. John with this passage.

Here is Peter with the other apostles, eating with Jesus. Christ turns to Peter and asks him three consecutive times, "do you love me?" What is Christ doing here? Let's return to the original language of the New Testament and uncover one more insight about the true self.

The first two times that Jesus asks Peter if he loves him, John translates it as the Greek "agapao," meaning "high devoted love." However, the third time John translates Christ's question with the word "phileo" in questioning Peter. Phileo, in Greek, is a more humble word for love as in love for a friend. Jesus challenges Peter to love, to live in his true self. However, as always, Christ is gentle and compassionate. John's change of word usage from agapao to phileo is significant in what it tells us about our Lord and Savior, as well as what it suggests about how we travel toward our true selves.

Jesus knew how imperfect Peter was, and he knows our imperfections as well. He knew Peter was not capable, at that point, of agapic love, "high, devoted love," so Jesus in his infinite love met Peter where he was at. And Jesus challenges us in the same way. He starts by letting us experience him as a non-judgmental friend only later inviting us to higher realms of agapic love, always taking into consideration our particular capacities.

Discovering and living in our true selves is not easy! We must cooperate with God's grace, and consistently strive to live a disciplined life of love. We don't just wake up one morning and magically get "fixed" by Christ. Yet Jesus recognizes that our journey toward wholeness and holiness is done with "baby steps." He doesn't expect us to be perfect. . .but to be willing to stay in the process of loving.

Here is a crucial lesson for relating to self and others, also. Be gentle! No one experiences healing through harshness. If we hear harshness and perfectionism in our own "self-talk" or in our interactions with others, we need to pull back and re-group. Here are a few questions to ask ourselves in the peace and quiet of our own hearts.

Who are we striving to serve? Is it our loving Lord, who gently asks us to love within our limits, or is it someone else? A parent who was never satisfied, a boss who demands perfection, a spouse who compares us to others? The pull to meet others' expectations must be understood in the light of Jesus' words to Peter: phileo moving toward agapao.

What do the compulsive messages we are tempted to follow tell us about personal injuries in our selves? If there are experiences we've been injured by along the way, experiences we have not really looked at, time must be spent understanding the losses involved, and the feelings that need to be felt. This hard work of healing memories is most often accomplished in a loving, accepting, community: spiritual, therapeutic, or both.

Finally, we must ask ourselves if we are trying to do other's work for them. It is disastrous for us to cross over onto someone else's "side of the street," and attempt to control what can't be controlled.

How do we maintain a sense of personal limits? By taking our own "inventory". . .remembering that there is more than enough unfinished work in our own lives, striving to be true selves. Focus on the "log" in our own eyes, and not the "splinter" in our neighbor's. . .but, as Christ showed with Peter, focus with gentleness.

The true self is discovered and lived in as we fulfill the commands of Christ to love. . .love with the spirit of compassion toward self and others. . .in process, growing toward holiness.

## For Reflection

1. In what ways do you already love Jesus very much in terms of friendship or high self-giving?

2. Who are the lambs Christ calls you to feed? What is the food you are called to give out of your true self?

3. What are areas in which you are harsh toward self and others?

4. How are you working on addressing unhealed parts of yourself that lead to fear and harshness?

### *Guided Imagery*

You are in one of the places where you find it easiest to sense the presence of Christ. You hear Jesus call you by name: (Susan, Jim, Lisa . . .) do you love me?

What does his question evoke in your head? Shame? Exaltation? Uncertainty? Challenge? Try to name the feeling.

He is showing you a vast array of "sheep." Who are these sheep? Name them. He asks you if you are willing to "feed" them.

What do you feel?

He asks you if you will be more willing if he agrees to do everything with you, side by side. You look up at him tentatively. He puts his arm around your shoulder and you walk together toward the sheep.

# Closing

*Healing Meditations From the Gospel of St. John: The Psychological and Spiritual Search for the True Self* is an exploratory book. As we wrote it we brought to it problem areas in our lives. We looked in the Gospel passages for clues to rebirth in our true selves, to freedom of spirit.

Often while creating a guided image with the help of the Holy Spirit we felt a foretaste in a momentary sense of healing that could give us hope for a future state where that peace would become characteristic of our daily feeling about our lives as Christians.

Sometimes when we came together to write a chapter, one of us or both would happen to be in a state of anxiety about something going on outside us and inside us that brought misery, depression, and hopeless feelings. We would feel a bit ashamed not to be at our best. Then we would remember that friendship does not come from performing well but from sharing vulnerability and bringing to each other and to the reader a compassionate heart. Astoundingly often the area of difficulty would come to healing through the graces Christ sent us as we prayed for each other.

We began to see the guided image like a northern star

to give light from far away which we could see even at those dark times when things seemed too grim to even want to invite Jesus to share with us. At such times we realized that it was not the time to try to force beautiful ideas to come forth, but rather to turn inwardly toward the place of peace, saying the Jesus prayer, the Our Father, Come, Holy Spirit, or the Hail Mary until we had become centered enough to seek insight.

After all, our salvation is not in writing or reading books but in the loving person of Christ accompanied by his cloud of witnesses: Mary, Joseph, the angels and saints, and all beloved folk who have gone before us fighting the good fight to the end.

And so we suggest that you take up this book from time to time again, letting the words of the Gospel of St. John come to you with the special focus of healing of the wounded self that you may come forth just a little bit stronger in grace, just a little bit more eager to risk moving out to God and those he sends as the true self God made, redeemed, and being sanctified daily.

AMEN

# To order additional copies of this book:

Please complete the form below and send for each copy

**CMJ Marian Publishers**
**P.O. Box 661 • Oak Lawn, IL 60454**
**toll free 888-636-6799**
**call 708-636-2995 or fax 708-636-2855**

**email jwby@aol.com**
**www.cmjbooks.com**

Name _____

Address _____

City _____ State ____ Zip _____

Phone (    ) _____

|  | QUANTITY | | SUBTOTAL |
|---|---|---|---|
| **The Grunt Padre**(hardcover) | | | |
| $22.95 each | x _____ | = | $ _____ |
| **The Grunt Padre**(softcover) | | | |
| $15.95 each | x _____ | = | $ _____ |
| **Radiating Christ** | | | |
| $11.00 each | x _____ | = | $ _____ |
| **Feminine, Free and Faithful** | | | |
| $9.95 each | x _____ | = | $ _____ |
| **Becoming the Handmaid of the Lord** | | | |
| $13.75 each | x _____ | = | $ _____ |
| **The Lost Years** | | | |
| $11.95 each | x _____ | = | $ _____ |
| **The Cheese Stands Alone** | | | |
| $12.50 each | x _____ | = | $ _____ |
| **Our Lady of the Outfield** | | | |
| $10.95 each | x _____ | = | $ _____ |
| **Feminine, Free and Faithful** | | | |
| $9.95 each | x _____ | = | $ _____ |
| **Quotable Saints** | | | |
| $9.95 each | x _____ | = | $ _____ |
| **Holding Hands with God** | | | |
| $9.95 each | x _____ | = | $ _____ |
| + tax (for Illinois residents only) | | = | $ _____ |
| + 15% for S & H | | = | $ _____ |
| **TOTAL** | | = | $ _____ |

☐ Check # _____ ☐ Visa ☐ MasterCard    Exp. Date __/__/__

Card # _____

Signature _____